The Great Deceiver:

From Eden to 2025

1

The Great Deceiver: From Eden to 2025

Note to the Reader

Before you turn the next page, I want you to know something very clearly.

This book was not written out of anger. It was not written to judge, shame, or condemn. It was written because the truth matters. It was written because deception is real. It was written because I care deeply about your soul.

We are living in a time when the line between light and darkness has been blurred. Good is called evil. Evil is called good. Many are walking through life unaware of the enemy working behind the scenes confusing, twisting, tempting, and destroying.

This book exists to expose that enemy. Not just the idea of Satan, but the very real work he is doing right now in churches, in homes, in culture, and in minds. If you're willing to look at the world with spiritual eyes, you'll see it and once you see it, you can't ignore it.

This book will not be sugarcoated. It will not avoid hard truth. It will not stay silent just because someone may be offended. The stakes are too high. The war is too real and too many are already falling.

But know this, this book is also full of hope. Real hope. The kind of hope that can only come from the truth of God's Word and the power of Jesus Christ. The goal here is not to scare you. The goal is to wake you up. To open your eyes. To help you walk in truth and to break free from any lie the enemy has wrapped around your life.

If you read these chapters with humility, with an open Bible, and with a sincere heart, I believe God will speak to you. He may challenge you. He may convict you. But He will always lead you in love.

Truth is not comfortable. But it is life-saving.

The deceiver is real. The danger is serious. But the truth still sets people free.

Thank you for being willing to read. Thank you for not turning away. My prayer is that by the time you reach the end, you will not just understand the battle we all face but you will be equipped to stand in victory.

For   His   glory,

Andy

4

Introduction

Why This Book Matters Now

"Take heed that no one deceives you. For many will come in My name... and will deceive many."

— Matthew 24:4–5

We are living in the age of deception.

The lines between truth and lies have blurred. What was once called evil is now celebrated. What was once holy is now mocked. The voices of false teachers fill the airwaves. The systems of the world grow darker by the day and behind it all moves one ancient enemy, the great deceiver.

His name is Satan. He is not a metaphor. He is not a fairy tale. He is not red with horns and a pitchfork. He is real. He is strategic. He is powerful. And he is working harder than ever to blind minds, twist truth, and lead souls to destruction.

This book was not written to entertain. It was not written to soften hearts or avoid offense. It was written to expose the works of darkness and call people back to the truth.

"For   we   are   not   ignorant   of   his   devices."

— 2 Corinthians 2:11

From the garden of Eden to the chaos of 2025, Satan's tactics have remained rooted in lies. But while his mission has not changed, his methods have multiplied. Technology, religion, culture, entertainment, education, and even churches have become battlegrounds for deception. And the greatest tragedy is that many do not see it.

Some are asleep. Others are compromised. Many are walking in a version of faith that has been stripped of power and truth.

This book will name the deceiver. It will trace his strategies through history. It will expose how he operates today and it will show you how to resist him not through fear, but through faith in Jesus Christ.

You will not find speculation here. You will not find conspiracy. You will find Scripture. You will find clarity. You will find urgency. And if you let it, you will find conviction that leads to freedom.

We cannot afford to be silent. We cannot afford to be passive. The war for truth is not coming, it is here.

7

Now is the time to wake up. Now is the time to return to the Word of God. Now is the time to put on the armor of God, to walk in discernment, to recognize the voice of the enemy, and to declare war on every lie that has taken root in our lives, our families, and our churches.

There is no middle ground. You will either walk in truth or be swept away by deception.

Let the Spirit of God open your eyes. Let the Word of God anchor your soul.

Let the deceiver be exposed.

Chapter 1: The First Lie

"Did God Really Say?"

"Now the serpent was more cunning than any beast of the field which the Lord God had made. And he said to the woman, 'Has God indeed said, "You shall not eat of every tree of the garden"?'"

— Genesis 3:1

Before there was sin, there was a lie. Before there was death, there was doubt. Before humanity ever tasted rebellion, it was deception that cracked the door.

The first recorded words of Satan in Scripture are not a declaration, a curse, or even a temptation. They are a question.

"Did God really say?"

That is where all deception begins. Not with a fiery threat, but with a whisper that causes you to second-guess the voice of the One who made you.

The Voice in the Garden

In the garden of Eden, God gave Adam and Eve every tree to enjoy, except one. It was not about withholding good. It was about preserving trust. Love is proven by choice, and trust is revealed through obedience. But Satan slithered into paradise with a purpose.

The Bible says the serpent was more cunning than any other creature. Cunning means subtle, crafty, skilled in manipulation. He did not come with fangs and fury. He came with a question that sounded innocent.

"Did God really say?"

Not "God is evil." Not "God is lying." Not "Go sin." Just a little twist. A slight bend. Enough to make Eve wonder if perhaps she misunderstood God's command.

Satan's strategy hasn't changed. He still begins by causing people to doubt the Word of God. He asks the same question in new forms.

- Did God really say marriage is between a man and a woman?
- Did God really say there is only one way to heaven?
- Did God really say you must repent?

- Did God really say judgment is real?
- Did God really say sin is still sin?

And once the question is asked, the erosion begins.

Twisting the Truth

After raising doubt, the serpent goes further. He adds just enough distortion to make the lie sound true.

"You will not surely die," the serpent said to the woman. "For God knows that in the day you eat of it your eyes will be opened, and you will be like God, knowing good and evil." — Genesis 3:4–5

Satan says, in effect, "God is holding you back. He knows you can be more. He's limiting your potential. Take control. Decide for yourself what is right and wrong. Be your own god."

That is the heart of deception: it takes God off the throne and puts you on it.

The enemy always wraps rebellion in something that sounds reasonable. He makes sin look wise. He makes pride feel empowering. He makes disobedience seem like growth.

This is not just ancient history. This is the same lie whispered in lecture halls, entertainment, pulpits, and personal hearts. Every false religion, every corrupt philosophy, every counterfeit gospel finds its origin in this one satanic idea:

"You can be like God."

It is the original humanism. The exaltation of self. The worship of one's own desires and opinions above God's Word.

And it always leads to death.

Eyes Opened, Souls Shattered

Eve ate. Adam followed. And just like that, paradise was broken.

Their eyes were opened, yes. But not to glory. Not to divine understanding. Their eyes were opened to shame, fear, and separation from God.

What Satan promised as freedom led to slavery. What he offered as wisdom led to confusion. What he claimed would elevate them actually brought them lower than they had ever been.

This is the fruit of deception. It always promises what it cannot deliver and delivers what it never promised.

The Liar Has Not Changed

In 2025, the same liar speaks. But now he has more voices. He speaks through media, through culture, through influencers, through false teachers, through compromised churches, and even through the silence of those who should be speaking truth.

He still asks the same question.

"Did God really say?"

He still twists Scripture. He still appeals to pride. He still tells people they can define truth for themselves.

And the tragedy is, many still believe him.

He has moved from the garden to the government. From the wilderness to the screen. From the snake to the smartphone. But the mission has not changed.

Satan does not need to burn down churches. He just needs to make the people inside them question what God said.

The Remedy for the Lie

There is only one weapon strong enough to expose and defeat the lie.

Truth.

"Your word is truth." — John 17:17

"You shall know the truth, and the truth shall make you free." — John 8:32

Truth is not a feeling. Truth is not a trend. Truth is not a social construct. Truth is a Person, and His name is Jesus.

To know the truth, you must know the Word of God. To resist deception, you must be grounded in Scripture. Satan cannot be overcome by emotions, opinions, or experiences. He must be overcome the same way Jesus overcame him in the wilderness.

"It is written."

This book will expose the deceiver for what he is. But more importantly, it will show you how to stand in truth. Not just to survive but to resist, to fight, and to overcome.

But it starts with seeing clearly.

You must stop asking, "Did God really say?" and start declaring, "God has said."

Because He has. And what He said is forever true.

Chapter 2: The Fall of Light

From Lucifer to the Father of Lies

"How you are fallen from heaven, O Lucifer, son of the morning! How you are cut down to the ground, you who weakened the nations!"
— Isaiah 14:12

He was not always the enemy. The one we now call Satan was once a radiant being, known as Lucifer. He walked among the stones of fire. He was anointed. Beautiful. Wise. Blameless.

Until pride was found in him.

The greatest deceiver in history began with the greatest fall. And before he ever deceived humanity, he deceived himself.

The Rise of Lucifer

The Bible pulls back the curtain on this mysterious figure in passages like Isaiah 14 and Ezekiel 28. Though written to earthly kings, these chapters seem to speak far beyond any human ruler. They describe a being whose glory once reflected the glory of God.

"You were the seal of perfection, full of wisdom and perfect in beauty. You were in Eden, the garden of God... You were the anointed cherub who covers... You were perfect in your ways from the day you were created, till iniquity · was found in you."
— Ezekiel 28:12–15

Lucifer was not equal to God. He was a created being, a high-ranking angel. His role may have been priestly, even musical. Some believe he was responsible for leading worship before the throne of God. But something happened in his heart.

He stopped reflecting the light and wanted to become the source of it.

The Five "I Wills"

Isaiah 14 reveals the inner corruption of Lucifer's heart. He wanted the throne, not the worship. He wanted to rise, not bow. He wanted to be above, not beneath.

"I will ascend into heaven."

"I will exalt my throne above the stars of God."

"I will sit on the mount of the congregation."

"I will ascend above the heights of the clouds."

"I will be like the Most High."

This is not ambition. This is rebellion.

Lucifer, in perfect beauty, desired something that was never his. He wanted to be like God. He wanted to dethrone the Almighty.

And just as quickly as the thought rose in his heart, he was cast down.

"You shall be brought down to Sheol, to the lowest depths of the Pit."
— Isaiah 14:15

What made Lucifer fall was not weakness. It was pride. The desire to rise above God is what turned an angel into a devil. That is why pride is still the favorite tool of the deceiver today.

The War in Heaven

Revelation 12 describes a cosmic war.

"And war broke out in heaven: Michael and his angels fought with the dragon... But they did not prevail, nor was a place found for them in heaven any longer. So the great dragon was cast out... He was cast to the earth, and his angels were cast out with him."
— Revelation 12:7–9

Lucifer's fall was not a solo descent. He took others with him. One third of the angels, seduced by his deception, joined his rebellion. They became what we now call demons.

It was the first great divide in creation. Heaven split. Glory turned to darkness. Worship turned to war.

And Satan was exiled to Earth, furious, defeated, but not yet destroyed.

From Light Bearer to Deceiver

The name Lucifer means "light bearer" or "morning star." But once he fell, he became the adversary—Satan. The accuser. The dragon. The old serpent. The god of this world. The prince of the power of the air.

He still wears disguises. He still pretends to be light.

"Satan himself transforms himself into an angel of light."
— 2 Corinthians 11:14

Do not think for a moment that evil always looks evil. The enemy is cunning. He wears beauty like a mask. He does not always come with horns. He often comes with charm. He will quote Scripture. He will use truth if it helps him twist the end.

He is not just the enemy of God. He is the enemy of your soul.

The Lie He Told Himself

Before Satan ever lied to Eve, he lied to himself.

He believed he could replace God. He believed he deserved worship. He believed his beauty, power, and position entitled him to rule.

That self-deception became a mission of mass deception. Now he whispers to humanity the same lie that ruined him.

"You can be your own god."

That is why pride is the root of all sin. It reflects the heart of Lucifer. It says, "I don't need to submit. I don't need God's Word. I will ascend. I will decide. I will rule."

But pride always comes before a fall.

Still Falling

Satan has already fallen, but he is not finished. He was cast from heaven. One day he will be cast into hell. But for now, he roams the earth with one goal, destruction.

"Your adversary the devil walks about like a roaring lion, seeking whom he may devour."
— 1 Peter 5:8

He is furious. He is focused. He is not playing games. He has seen the glory of God. He knows he can never have it. So now he seeks to keep others from it.

He hates humanity because we were made in the image of the God he tried to overthrow. You are not the center of the story, but you are part of the battlefield. Satan wants your mind, your marriage, your children, your soul. He wants churches powerless and preachers silent. He wants the truth questioned and sin embraced.

His fall was only the beginning. His war continues. And the battlefield is right in front of you.

The Light Still Shines

Lucifer fell. Satan fights. But Jesus reigns.

He is the true Morning Star. He is the Light of the World. He is the One the devil cannot dethrone.

The only way to stand in this present darkness is to walk in that light.

This book is not just about exposing the deceiver. It is about pointing you to the Deliverer.

Satan has fallen. Truth has risen.

And light always wins.

Chapter 3: The Pattern of Deception

Old Tactics. New Targets.

"You are of your father the devil, and the desires of your father you want to do. He was a murderer from the beginning, and does not stand in the truth... When he speaks a lie, he speaks from his own resources, for he is a liar and the father of it."
— John 8:44

Satan has no need to invent new lies. He only needs to perfect the old ones. Every generation thinks they are facing something new, but the truth is, the enemy has been using the same core tactics since Eden. He simply dresses them in new language.

He does not need to change the strategy. He just needs to change the setting.

And if you cannot recognize the pattern, you will fall for it every time.

The Blueprint for Deception

Satan has a method. His moves are not random. He operates with purpose. The Bible reveals his tactics, and they form a clear pattern repeated throughout history:

1. **Question God's Word**
2. **Twist God's Truth**
3. **Appeal to Pride or Pleasure**
4. **Offer a Shortcut**
5. **Distract from the Consequences**

That is how he deceived Eve. That is how he tempted Jesus. That is how he corrupts the Church. That is how he blinds the lost.

His pattern is predictable—but deadly.

Step One: Question God's Word

As we saw in the garden, Satan begins with doubt.

"Has God indeed said...?"

He does not demand rebellion. He just raises uncertainty. If he can make someone question the authority or clarity of God's Word, the door opens. A person who doubts the Word will soon defy the Word.

Today, the question has taken on new forms:

- Is the Bible really reliable?
- Isn't Scripture just a product of culture?
- Doesn't everyone interpret it differently?
- Isn't love more important than doctrine?

The enemy does not shout these doubts. He plants them quietly, in the hearts of students, leaders, and even pastors. Then he waits for the roots to grow.

Step Two: Twist the Truth

Once the truth is questioned, Satan twists it. He rarely denies God's Word outright. He simply bends it.

He quoted Scripture when he tempted Jesus. But he left out part of the verse. He changed the context. He used God's Word as a weapon against the Son of God.

Satan loves half-truths. A half-truth can destroy just as completely as a full lie.

Today, the twisting sounds like this:

- God wants you to be happy.
- Grace means sin doesn't matter.
- Jesus didn't talk about that issue, so it must be okay.
- Everyone sins, so who are you to judge?

This is deception wrapped in religious language. It sounds spiritual, but it leads away from the Spirit.

Step Three: Appeal to Pride or Pleasure

The devil knows how to bait the hook. He appeals to the flesh. He whispers to the ego. "You will be like God."

It is always about power, pleasure, or self. The world says, "Do what feels right." The enemy says, "Follow your heart." But the Bible says the heart is deceitful.

Satan feeds our desire to control, to be praised, to indulge, to justify.

Whether it is a forbidden fruit, a secret sin, or a false identity, the goal is the same: to make you trust yourself more than you trust God.

Step Four: Offer a Shortcut

The enemy knows people want results without obedience. He offers success without surrender, power without purity, glory without a cross.

He told Jesus to turn stones into bread, to throw Himself from the temple, to worship him and receive the kingdoms of the world.

All shortcuts. All lies.

Satan will always offer what looks like a quicker way to fulfillment. But every shortcut he offers leads away from the path of life.

Step Five: Hide the Consequences

Sin always comes with a price. But Satan hides the receipt.

"You will not surely die."

That was the first outright lie. He promised Eve there would be no judgment, no consequences. Just freedom and enlightenment.

It is the same lie today.

- Live your truth. No judgment.
- God understands. It is not a big deal.
- Everyone does it.
- You're still a good person.

He promises that sin will satisfy. But he never shows what it costs. The pain. The shame. The addiction. The separation from God. The spiritual death.

The Target: Your Mind

The battlefield is not just in culture. It is in your mind.

"The god of this world has blinded the minds of those who do not believe."
— 2 Corinthians 4:4

Satan does not need to chain your body if he can cloud your thinking. If he can change the way you see truth, he can control how you live. That is why the renewing of the mind is so critical. That is why Scripture must saturate your soul.

The devil's primary weapon is deception. And your primary defense is truth.

Recognizing the Pattern

If you know the pattern, you can see it coming. You will begin to recognize the whispers.

You will hear the lie under the surface. You will spot the shortcut for what it is.

Satan's methods are old. But they still work on hearts that do not know the truth.

He will never stop trying to deceive. But you do not have to keep falling for it.

Stand firm. Know the Word. Walk in the light.

And never forget the devil has a pattern, but your God has a plan.

Chapter 4: The Deceiver in the Old World

Before the Flood and the Tower of Babel

"Then the Lord saw that the wickedness of man was great in the earth, and that every intent of the thoughts of his heart was only evil continually."
— Genesis 6:5

The world did not begin in chaos. It began in beauty. A garden. A command. A Creator walking with man in the cool of the day. But after the first lie, after the first fall, something began to spread. Like poison in the bloodstream, rebellion crept into every generation.

By the time of Noah, the world was not simply broken. It was consumed.

And behind the scenes, still slithering through human history, was the deceiver.

A World Gone Wild

After Cain killed Abel, sin began to multiply. The descendants of Cain built cities and pursued their own greatness. Violence filled the earth. Idolatry took root. Immorality exploded. And while people blamed human nature or the passage of time, they missed the influence of something darker.

Satan was not idle. He was building momentum. His mission to destroy humanity did not stop at the garden gate. It expanded.

"The earth also was corrupt before God, and the earth was filled with violence."
— Genesis 6:11

What caused such deep and widespread corruption? Scripture gives us a glimpse of something supernatural, something beyond the surface of history.

The Sons of God and the Daughters of Men

"That the sons of God saw the daughters of men, that they were beautiful; and they took wives for themselves of all whom they chose."
— Genesis 6:2

This mysterious passage has sparked debate for centuries. But one thing is clear—something unholy occurred. Whether these "sons of God" were fallen angels or powerful men influenced by the demonic, the result was a world so wicked that God was grieved He had made man.

The enemy was actively working to corrupt the bloodline, defile creation, and stop the promise of a coming Savior. That was always his goal.

He heard the prophecy in the garden.

"I will put enmity between you and the woman, and between your seed and her Seed."
— Genesis 3:15

Satan knew a Redeemer was coming. A Seed would crush his head. So from the beginning, he tried to prevent it. First through murder. Then through corruption. Then through deception and destruction.

If he could ruin the people, he could stop the promise.

A Righteous Man in a Rotten World

But God always has a remnant. In the middle of the madness, one man stood out.

"Noah was a just man, perfect in his generations. Noah walked with God."
— Genesis 6:9

Noah was not perfect in the modern sense. But he was uncorrupted. Faithful. Obedient.
God gave him a mission that seemed insane, build an ark when there had been no rain.
And Noah obeyed.

For 120 years, he built and preached. A preacher of righteousness in a world of violence and lust. Satan scoffed. The people mocked. But God was not joking.

When the rain came, it did not stop. The judgment was not symbolic. It was total.

The flood wiped the earth clean. But Satan was not done.

Babel and the Birth of Rebellion

After the flood, humanity began again. But the heart had not changed. Sin remained. And once again, the deceiver stirred the people toward pride.

"Come, let us build ourselves a city, and a tower whose top is in the heavens; let us make a   name   for   ourselves."
— Genesis 11:4

This was not architecture. This was arrogance. The tower of Babel was humanity's declaration of independence from God. It was a monument to self-worship. A collective rebellion and behind it was the same voice that whispered in the garden.

"You will be like God."

The people wanted unity, but without submission. They wanted greatness, but without righteousness. They wanted heaven, but without the King of Heaven.

Satan was building a system. A global rebellion. A counterfeit kingdom.

But God confused their language. He scattered their plans. The tower stood unfinished. The enemy's reach was delayed, but not destroyed.

The Pattern Continues

In the days before the flood, Satan corrupted the people. After the flood, he inspired their pride. The same deception, different form. Chaos, then control.

That is still his goal today.

- Corrupt the heart through sin.
- Unite the world in rebellion.
- Build a godless kingdom.
- Replace worship with domination.

The spirit of Babel lives on. In globalism without God. In systems that exalt man. In movements that silence the Word. In ideologies that erase truth.

And Satan still whispers the same words:

"Make a name for yourself."

God Still Rules

Though the world was violent, God preserved Noah. Though the tower rose, God scattered the builders. Though the enemy plotted, God's plan advanced.

He called Abraham. He formed Israel. He prepared the way for Christ.

Satan's kingdom has always been temporary. God's kingdom is eternal.

And every time the deceiver tries to rise, God steps in. The flood was not the end. The scattering at Babel was not the solution. But they were signs.

God sees. God judges. God intervenes.

And the devil is always on a leash.

The Battle Lines Are Clear

You must decide where you stand. You will either be part of the remnant or the rebellion. You will either walk with God like Noah or build with pride like Babel.

This war is not new. The patterns are ancient. But the stakes are eternal.

The deceiver still moves. But so does the Spirit of God.

And the time to choose is now.

Chapter 5: Counterfeit Religion and False Worship

When Evil Wears Robes

"They served their idols, which became a snare to them. They even sacrificed their sons and their daughters to demons."
— Psalm 106:36–37

Satan does not mind religion. In fact, he thrives in it. He does not care if people gather in buildings, sing songs, or speak spiritual words, as long as their hearts are far from God.

If he cannot keep people from worshiping, he will twist their worship. If he cannot destroy their faith, he will counterfeit it. If he cannot stop the name of God from being spoken, he will pollute what that name means.

The enemy has never stopped promoting false worship. He just learned how to dress it up in religious robes.

The God Who Is Not God

From the very beginning, Satan has been a master counterfeiter. He does not create. He corrupts. He takes what is holy and makes it hollow. He takes what is true and makes it toxic.

The golden calf was not just an idol. It was a substitute for the living God. The people in the wilderness still claimed to worship "the Lord." But they made Him in their own image. *"This is your god, O Israel, that brought you out of the land of Egypt!"*
— Exodus 32:4

They did not stop worshiping. They just started worshiping wrongly.

This is the essence of counterfeit religion. It keeps the form but loses the fire. It uses God's name but denies His nature. It feels sacred, but it leads to destruction.

Baal, Asherah, and the Prophets of Lies

Throughout Israel's history, the people were constantly tempted to follow the gods of the nations. Baal. Asherah. Molech. Chemosh. These were not just carved images. They represented spiritual strongholds. Demonic influences.

"They forsook the Lord and served Baal and the Ashtoreths."
— Judges 2:13

These religions offered pleasure, prosperity, and power. They demanded sacrifices, even human ones. And behind their altars stood the deceiver.

False prophets multiplied. Altars rose. The people bowed to gods who were no gods at all.

"The things which the Gentiles sacrifice they sacrifice to demons and not to God."
— 1 Corinthians 10:20

Satan does not need people to worship him directly. He just needs them to worship anything other than the one true God.

Religious Leaders, Not Just Pagan Priests

The enemy does not only influence foreign temples. He works within God's people. Some of the most dangerous voices in Scripture wore priestly garments and claimed to speak for the Lord.

- The sons of Eli corrupted the priesthood with immorality and greed.
- The false prophets of Jeremiah's day told people peace was coming when judgment was near.
- The Pharisees in Jesus' day turned the faith into a burden and used the Law to crush instead of restore.

Jesus did not just confront sinners. He confronted religious men who thought they represented God.

"You are of your father the devil... He was a murderer from the beginning... When he speaks a lie, he speaks from his own resources."
— John 8:44

The enemy knows that false religion is often more effective than open rebellion. It deceives the heart while appearing holy. It hardens the conscience while keeping the ritual.

Modern Idols, Same Old Spirit

Today, most people do not bow before statues. But that does not mean they are not worshiping idols. Anything placed above God becomes an object of worship. Anything that replaces obedience becomes a false religion.

- Prosperity without purity

- Grace without repentance
- Worship without surrender
- Spirituality without truth

These are the new altars. These are the false gods of today.

Modern counterfeit religion says:

- "As long as you're sincere, you're safe."
- "God just wants you to be happy."
- "All paths lead to the same place."
- "Jesus is love, but not Lord."

Satan does not care if people call it church, as long as it is powerless. He does not care if they read Scripture, as long as they twist it. He does not care if they sing songs, as long as their hearts are chasing something else.

The Warning to the Church

In the book of Revelation, Jesus warned seven churches. Some were faithful. Others had compromised. One in particular had embraced counterfeit religion.

"You have there those who hold the doctrine of Balaam... who taught Balak to put a stumbling block before the children of Israel." — Revelation 2:14

This was spiritual compromise hidden behind religious words. It was sin in the sanctuary. Tolerance of lies in the name of love.

Jesus did not commend it. He threatened to fight against it.

He is not looking for religion. He is looking for truth and fire. Spirit and truth. A people who love Him more than tradition, culture, or comfort.

Testing the Spirits

The Bible tells us not to believe every voice, not to trust every teacher.

"Beloved, do not believe every spirit, but test the spirits, whether they are of God... because many false prophets have gone out into the world." — 1 John 4:1

If it contradicts Scripture, it is not of God. If it excuses sin, it is not of God. If it denies the cross, the resurrection, or the Lordship of Christ, it is not of God.

No matter how charming the speaker is. No matter how large the crowd. No matter how powerful the emotions.

Satan still wears robes. He still quotes Scripture. He still sits in religious seats of power. But his heart is filled with lies.

Worship the Right Way

God is not looking for perfect people. He is looking for surrendered ones. The kind of worship that pleases Him is not built on talent or tradition. It is built on truth.

"The true worshipers will worship the Father in spirit and truth." — John 4:23

If the enemy can get you to worship a false god or follow a false gospel, he has already won the battle for your soul.

So test what you hear. Measure what you believe. Know the difference between what is holy and what only looks like it.

Satan is not against religion. He just wants it to be counterfeit.

Let your worship be real. Let your faith be true. Let your heart belong to Christ alone.

Chapter 6: The Temptation of Christ

Confronting the Liar Face to Face

"Then Jesus was led up by the Spirit into the wilderness to be tempted by the devil."
— Matthew 4:1

In the garden, the first Adam fell. In the wilderness, the second Adam stood.

Satan had succeeded in deceiving humanity, corrupting worship, twisting truth, and spreading death. But now, for the first time in recorded history, he faced a man who could not be deceived.

Not just a man, but the Son of God in flesh. Jesus Christ. Fully man. Fully God. And He came not just to die for sin, but to defeat the one who caused it.

The showdown in the wilderness was not just about temptation. It was a direct confrontation between the deceiver and the Deliverer. It was a moment where the lies of hell collided with the truth of heaven.

Led into Battle

Jesus had just been baptized. The Spirit descended. The Father spoke from heaven, declaring His pleasure in the Son. It was a moment of public affirmation. A divine anointing.

And immediately after, the Spirit led Jesus into the wilderness.

Not to rest. Not to preach. But to be tested.

This was not a mistake. It was part of the mission. Before Jesus stepped into public ministry, He would face the enemy head-on. Not in a palace, but in a barren desert. Not with angels singing, but with hunger gnawing. Not with followers, but in complete isolation.

The enemy always attacks in weakness. But Jesus was never vulnerable. He was prepared.

The First Temptation: Physical Need

"If You are the Son of God, command that these stones become bread."
— Matthew 4:3

Jesus had fasted for forty days. He was hungry. Satan saw an opportunity.

"If You are the Son of God..."

Here comes the doubt again. Just like in the garden. Just like at Babel. Challenge the identity. Question the Word. Twist the moment.

Satan knew who Jesus was. He had seen His glory before the world began. But he wanted Jesus to prove it by misusing His power to satisfy His flesh.

But Jesus replied,

"It is written, 'Man shall not live by bread alone, but by every word that proceeds from the mouth of God.'"

He did not argue. He did not perform. He quoted Scripture. That is how truth responds to deception.

The Second Temptation: Pride and Presumption

"If You are the Son of God, throw Yourself down... For it is written..." — Matthew 4:6

This time, Satan quotes Scripture. He uses Psalm 91. He tries to sound holy. He speaks in religious language.

But he leaves something out. He twists the meaning. He invites Jesus to test God instead of trust Him.

This is how false teachers operate. They use Scripture, but not truthfully. They make the Word a tool to manipulate God instead of a sword to fight the enemy.

Jesus responded again with the Word.

"It is written again, 'You shall not tempt the Lord your God.'"

He knew the full context. He did not fall for half-truths. He stayed grounded in the whole counsel of God.

The Third Temptation: Power Without the Cross

"All these things I will give You if You will fall down and worship me." — Matthew 4:9

Here Satan drops the mask. No more subtlety. No more twisted Scripture. Just a naked offer of power and glory.

He shows Jesus the kingdoms of the world. He offers influence, control, and dominion.

But there is a price. Worship.

Satan wanted what he had always wanted. The worship that belongs to God alone.

He tried to give Jesus the crown without the cross. He offered the reward without the suffering. But Jesus did not come to take a shortcut. He came to destroy the deceiver's system.

"Away with you, Satan! For it is written, 'You shall worship the Lord your God, and Him only you shall serve.'"

With that, the battle was won. The enemy left. Angels came. And Jesus stood victorious.

Why This Matters Now

This was not just about Jesus. It was about you. This moment in the wilderness shows how Satan tempts, how truth defeats, and how we are to fight.

Satan still uses the same tactics today.

- He tempts you through the flesh.
- He tempts you through pride.
- He tempts you through shortcuts.

And in every case, Jesus shows us the response.

Stand on Scripture.

Trust God's timing.

Refuse to worship anything but the Father.

Jesus did not win by miracles. He won by obedience. He overcame with the Word, not with displays of power.

If Jesus, the Son of God, used the Word to resist the devil, how much more should we?

The Sword of the Spirit

Ephesians 6 calls the Word of God the sword of the Spirit. Not a decorative weapon. Not a book to sit on a shelf. A weapon for war.

You cannot fight deception with opinions. You cannot resist temptation with feelings. You must know the Word. Speak the Word. Stand on the Word.

Satan knows Scripture. But he cannot stand against it when it is spoken in truth.

The Battle Is Personal

You will face your own wilderness moments. Times of weakness. Times of testing. Times when the enemy whispers doubt, offers false comfort, or promises something that seems good but pulls you away from God.

Remember the pattern. Remember the Word.

Jesus was tempted in every way, yet without sin. He knows your struggle. He stands with you. And He has already overcome the one who seeks to destroy you.

You are not fighting for victory. You are fighting from it.

The deceiver still prowls. But the truth still stands.

And the One who overcame him in the wilderness now lives in you.

Chapter 7: Deception in the Early Church

Wolves Among the Sheep

"For I know this, that after my departure savage wolves will come in among you, not sparing the flock. Also from among yourselves men will rise up, speaking perverse things, to draw away the disciples after themselves."
— Acts 20:29–30

The early Church was born in fire. Miracles flowed. Thousands were saved. The gospel spread like wildfire across cities, nations, and empires.

But wherever God builds, Satan tries to break.

The devil could not stop the resurrection, so he targeted the result. If he could not kill Christ, he would try to corrupt the Church. And he did not always do it with violence. He used deception.

The wolves did not howl from the outside. They crept in from within.

Ananias and Sapphira: The First Church Scandal

In Acts chapter 5, we see deception appear early.

Ananias and Sapphira sold land and pretended to give all the money to the Church. They lied. Not just to Peter. Not just to the people. But to the Holy Spirit.

Their sin was not withholding money. Their sin was presenting themselves as more spiritual than they truly were.

Hypocrisy is a form of deception. It looks holy. It acts generous. But it hides a false heart.

Peter called them out with a bold statement.

"Why has Satan filled your heart to lie to the Holy Spirit?"

Satan had found an opening. Not through persecution. Through pride. Through dishonesty. Through fake devotion. He knows that if he can't destroy a church from the outside, he'll do it from the inside.

God responded swiftly. Both Ananias and Sapphira fell dead. It was not just judgment. It was a warning.

God will not tolerate deception among His people.

False Teachers and Counterfeit Gospels

As the gospel spread, so did opposition. Paul, Peter, John, and Jude all warned of those who would twist the message and lead others astray.

"For such are false apostles, deceitful workers, transforming themselves into apostles of Christ."

— 2 Corinthians 11:13

Some came with charisma. Some came with credentials. Some came with legalism. Others came with license to sin.

But all of them carried the same goal: to corrupt the gospel.

In Galatians, Paul did not mince words.

"But even if we, or an angel from heaven, preach any other gospel… let him be accursed."

That is the strength of the warning. There is one gospel. One truth. One cross. And anyone who twists it is not sent by God.

They may speak well. They may gather crowds. They may look like sheep.

But they are wolves.

The Spirit of Antichrist

John wrote to warn the Church of an even deeper threat, the spirit of antichrist. Not just opposition to Christ, but replacement of Christ.

"Every spirit that does not confess that Jesus Christ has come in the flesh is not of God."

— 1 John 4:3

The early Church faced this deception often. Some denied that Jesus was truly God. Others claimed He was God but not truly man. These lies eroded the foundation of the faith.

Satan does not always try to remove Jesus from the picture. He just tries to distort Him. A distorted Christ cannot save. A counterfeit Jesus is no different from an idol.

The Church was not only battling the culture. It was battling corruption in the pulpit, confusion in doctrine, and compromise in leadership.

Doctrine Matters

In today's world, many say doctrine divides. That truth is personal. That theology is optional.

But the apostles did not see it that way.

Paul told Timothy to guard the doctrine. To fight for the truth. To silence those who were teaching error.

"Take heed to yourself and to the doctrine. Continue in them, for in doing this you will save both yourself and those who hear you." — 1 Timothy 4:16

What you believe about God shapes everything. If the enemy can twist your doctrine, he can warp your worship, your walk, and your witness.

The early Church survived because they held fast to the gospel. Not just the feeling of it, but the truth of it.

Satan's Strategy Then and Now

Satan's plan in the early Church is the same today.

- Insert lies where there should be truth
- Create division where there should be unity
- Elevate personality over purity
- Replace sound doctrine with smooth talk
- Use signs and wonders to distract from the Word

He uses familiar faces. Trusted voices. Spiritual language. But the goal is destruction.

The early Church was not immune. Neither are we.

The Call to Discernment

Not every preacher is sent by God. Not every church is led by the Spirit. Not every revival is from heaven.

This does not mean we live in fear or suspicion. It means we stay grounded in the Word. It means we test every spirit. It means we care more about truth than popularity.

The Holy Spirit gives discernment. The Word of God gives clarity. The Church must remain awake.

The deceiver got into the early Church. He is still trying today.

But truth still exposes lies. Light still scatters darkness. And Jesus still purifies His bride.

Chapter 8: The Great Lie in the Modern World

From Enlightenment to Entitlement

"Professing to be wise, they became fools, and changed the glory of the incorruptible God into an image made like corruptible man..."
— Romans 1:22–23

Every era has its idols. Every age carries its lies. But no deception is more dangerous than the one that says you no longer need God.

The lie is not always shouted. It is often embedded quietly in the culture, in education, in media, and even in churches. It is the lie that says truth is relative, morality is subjective, and man is the measure of all things.

This is not a new deception. It is simply the old rebellion of Eden dressed in modern clothing.

"You will be like God."

The modern world has embraced that line fully. And Satan, the great deceiver, smiles while the world praises itself.

The Rise of Humanism

During the Enlightenment, humanity began to exalt reason over revelation. Philosophers declared that man was no longer bound to ancient authority. Science became the new religion. God was pushed to the sidelines. The Bible was called outdated.

And slowly, culture replaced divine truth with self-made wisdom.

Humanism teaches that man is inherently good, self-sufficient, and progressing toward perfection. But Scripture says the heart is deceitful. The Word says all have sinned.

The deceiver knew that if he could shift the foundation from God to man, the whole structure would collapse. And it has.

Morality becomes personal. Authority becomes offensive. Salvation becomes unnecessary.

The Death of Truth

In the age of postmodernism, the lie evolved again.

Truth was no longer denied. It was deconstructed.

"Live   your   truth."

"Speak   your   truth."

"What's true for you may not be true for me."

This sounds freeing. It feels empowering. But it is poison.

If everyone has their own truth, then no one has *the* truth. And when that happens, the door opens wide for the deceiver to fill the void.

Satan thrives in confusion. He sows doubt. He multiplies voices. He promotes tolerance of every idea except the one that saves.

Jesus said,

"I am the way, the truth, and the life. No one comes to the Father except through Me."

But the world now says, "That's too narrow."

What used to be sin is now self-expression. What used to be conviction is now called hate. What used to be gospel is now seen as judgment.

The deceiver has not stopped attacking truth. He has simply learned how to make people comfortable without it.

Entitlement and the Worship of Self

The modern world no longer bows to carved idols. It bows to self.

Self-care has replaced self-denial. Self-expression has replaced surrender. Feelings have become kings. And God is seen as a distant idea, not a present Lord.

This is not just cultural. It is deeply spiritual.

"In the last days perilous times will come: for men will be lovers of themselves..."
— 2 Timothy 3:1–2

The heart of modern deception is not rebellion with fists raised. It is comfort with eyes closed. It is spiritual apathy. Moral compromise. Emotional flattery.

The devil is not trying to terrify everyone. He is trying to tranquilize them. He wants people entertained, numbed, distracted, and deceived.

And if he can keep them obsessed with themselves, he can keep them from seeing the truth.

The Illusion of Progress

The world celebrates advancement. More technology. More science. More access to information.

But none of it brings peace to the soul.

Depression has skyrocketed. Anxiety is everywhere. Identity is confused. Families are fractured. Morality is collapsing. And the deceiver whispers, "This is freedom."

But it is not freedom. It is a prison with invisible bars. It is rebellion without resistance.

Satan does not need the world to hate God. He just needs them to forget Him.

The Church's Silence

One of the most heartbreaking parts of this modern deception is the silence of the Church.

Many pulpits have traded the fear of God for the applause of men. Conviction has been replaced with comfort. Messages have become motivational rather than transformational.

When the Church stops preaching the truth, the world loses its last warning.

False gospels now thrive.

- The prosperity gospel says God exists to bless you.
- The progressive gospel says God approves of sin.
- The universalist gospel says everyone is saved no matter what.

Each one is wrapped in just enough Scripture to sound right. But each one is a lie.

And behind every lie is the father of lies.

The Time Is Now

We do not live in neutral times. These are days of spiritual war. Every screen, every voice, every worldview is either drawing people to truth or pulling them deeper into deception.

The great lie of our age is this:

"You don't need God. You are enough."

But that lie leads to death. It does not heal. It does not save. It does not satisfy.

Only truth can do that. Only Jesus can do that.

The deceiver has infected the modern world. But the truth still sets captives free.

You must open your eyes. You must speak the truth. You must stand in the light.

Because the enemy is not slowing down.

And the time to fight deception is now.

Chapter 9: Satan's 2025 Playbook

New Tools. Same Mission.

"The coming of the lawless one is according to the working of Satan, with all power, signs, and lying wonders, and with all unrighteous deception among those who perish, because they did not receive the love of the truth, that they might be saved."
— 2 Thessalonians 2:9–10

The devil does not need to change his mission. He only needs to update his methods. His goal remains the same: steal, kill, and destroy. His nature remains the same: liar, accuser, deceiver. But the battlefield has evolved, and so have his weapons.

This is not the same world that existed fifty years ago. This is not the same battlefield that the early Church faced. The year is 2025, and the deceiver has more tools than ever. They are subtle. They are sophisticated. They are everywhere.

And most people are too distracted, too entertained, or too afraid to notice.

What you are about to read may offend. It may even hurt. But truth does not comfort lies. It exposes them. And we will not win a spiritual war by pretending the enemy is not advancing.

It is time to unmask the modern playbook of the great deceiver.

1. Artificial Intelligence and Digital Deception

The rise of artificial intelligence is not neutral. AI can be used for good, but it is quickly becoming a tool for deep deception.

- AI-generated false sermons that sound biblical
- AI imitations of voices, faces, and religious leaders
- AI-fueled deepfakes spreading false signs and wonders
- Personalized heresy delivered through algorithms

What once required demonic possession now comes through data patterns. And people are believing lies created by machines.

Scripture warns of a time when deception would come with signs and wonders. That time is no longer future. It is present.

"Evil men and impostors will grow worse and worse, deceiving and being deceived."
— 2 Timothy 3:13

2. Progressive Christianity

Satan does not mind churches, he just wants them to preach a different gospel.

Progressive Christianity removes the offense of the cross. It denies the authority of Scripture. It replaces repentance with affirmation. It elevates social trends over eternal truth.

- Sin is redefined as self-expression.
- Holiness is seen as intolerance.
- Love is used to excuse lawlessness.

This is not Christianity. It is rebellion in robes. It is the serpent in the sanctuary.

"They will not endure sound doctrine... they will turn their ears away from the truth and be turned aside to fables."
— 2 Timothy 4:3–4

3. Gender Confusion and Identity Warfare

God made male and female. Satan wants to blur that line until it disappears.

Gender confusion is not just a social issue. It is spiritual war against the image of God. If the deceiver can distort identity, he can destroy calling, relationships, and generations.

Children are being targeted. Curriculums are being rewritten. Truth is now considered hate. And to even speak the created design of God is called discrimination.

This is not love. It is deception. And behind it is the one who always hates the image of God.

"God is not the author of confusion."
— 1 Corinthians 14:33

4. TikTok Prophets and Viral Heresies

Millions now get their theology from TikTok, Instagram, or YouTube. The most popular voices are not the most biblical, they are the most entertaining.

- Clips taken out of context.
- Preachers with no accountability.
- Prophets chasing views instead of truth.

Satan has weaponized attention spans. People no longer study the Word. They scroll through it in sixty seconds.

"By smooth words and flattering speech they deceive the hearts of the simple."
— Romans 16:18

5. New Age Practices in Christian Clothing

The world has embraced witchcraft as wellness. Astrology, energy healing, crystals, manifestation, and ancestral worship are now mainstream. Worse, these ideas are creeping into churches.

- "Speak it into existence"
- "Feel the universe guiding you"
- "Cleanse your energy"

None of this is biblical. All of it is demonic.

People do not need to align their chakras. They need to bow to the cross.

"What fellowship has righteousness with lawlessness? And what communion has light with   darkness?"
— 2 Corinthians 6:14

6. Entertainment as Indoctrination

The devil used to tempt from the shadows. Now he preaches through screens.

Hollywood normalizes perversion. Music promotes rebellion. Cartoons teach children that witches are heroes and demons are friends. Video games celebrate darkness and call it fun.

And the Church remains silent while families are discipled by Disney, Netflix, and Spotify.

This is not just about taste. It is about spiritual saturation. What you consume, you become.

"I   will   set   nothing   wicked   before   my   eyes."
— Psalm 101:3

7. Globalism Without God

There is a growing push for global unity, one government, one currency, one system, one belief. It sounds peaceful. It looks compassionate.

But it is setting the stage for control.

The Bible warns of a coming world leader, the Antichrist, who will deceive nations. What we are seeing now is the groundwork.

- Digital currencies that can be controlled
- Global health mandates
- International religious alliances without Christ

The world is uniting but not under Jesus. And that is no accident.

"The whole world marveled and followed the beast."
— Revelation 13:3

8. Censorship of Biblical Truth

Truth is now hate speech. Social media bans Scripture. Algorithms suppress sermons. Platforms silence anything that confronts sin.

Yet perversion is promoted. Blasphemy is celebrated. And pastors stay quiet, afraid to lose followers.

This is spiritual war. Not against people, but against principalities.

"They exchanged the truth of God for the lie."
— Romans 1:25

9. Digital Addiction and Mental Slavery

The average person cannot sit in silence for five minutes. Attention spans are destroyed. Stillness feels like suffering.

Why?

Because the deceiver wants a noisy mind. If you are always distracted, you will never hear the still, small voice of God.

Phones have become altars. Likes have become validation. And silence has become unbearable.

"Be still, and know that I am God."
— Psalm 46:10

10. False Unity Without Truth

There is a movement to bring all religions together—peace at the expense of truth.

"Let's focus on what we have in common."
"Let's stop dividing people with doctrine."

"Let's all worship the same God in different ways."

But Jesus is not one of many. He is the only way. Unity without Christ is not peace. It is preparation for deception.

"No one comes to the Father except through Me."
— John 14:6

The Deceiver Is Not Hiding

He is speaking through culture. He is moving through systems. He is shaping beliefs through content, personalities, and platforms.

And many are being swept away because they refuse to see it.

You cannot defeat what you will not name. You cannot resist what you refuse to acknowledge.

This chapter is not meant to stir fear. It is meant to shake off blindness. These are not conspiracy theories. They are spiritual realities confirmed by Scripture and visible in daily life.

The deceiver's playbook is not secret. It is public. It is praised. It is applauded.

But it will be judged.

Stand in the Truth

The answer is not retreat. It is resistance.

You must know the truth. Speak the truth. Live the truth. Raise your family in truth. Lead your church in truth. Guard your mind in truth.

The enemy is not sleeping. Neither can we.

This is 2025. The war is here. And the truth still sets captives free.

Chapter 10: The Deceived Church

Truth Compromised. Power Lost.

"Having a form of godliness but denying its power. And from such people turn away!"
— 2 Timothy 3:5

The Church is called to be the pillar and ground of truth. It is meant to be the salt of the earth, the light of the world, a holy bride prepared for her returning King.

But not all that calls itself church today carries the mark of Christ. Many buildings are filled. Many programs are funded. But the Spirit is not present.

Why?

Because deception has not just entered the world. It has entered the sanctuary. The deceiver has not only gone after governments and media. He has crept into pulpits, pews, worship songs, and leadership conferences.

And many churches are now preaching what Satan wants to hear.

The Sin of Silence

In a world drowning in confusion, the Church should be the clearest voice. But many pulpits have gone quiet.

- Silent on sin to avoid offense.
- Silent on judgment to protect attendance.
- Silent on holiness to remain relevant.

The devil does not need to close a church. He only needs to make it silent where it matters.
"They are blind guides. And if the blind lead the blind, both will fall into a ditch."
— Matthew 15:14

Truth that is not spoken is truth that cannot save. A gospel that does not confront sin is not the gospel. And a church that refuses to stand against deception will eventually serve it.

Entertained but Not Transformed

Some churches have traded reverence for performance. They draw crowds but not conviction. They create atmospheres but not disciples. They stir emotions but never expose idols.

Lights, fog machines, and gifted communicators do not guarantee the presence of God. Entertainment is not evil. But when it replaces holiness, it becomes idolatry.

The deceiver loves when people feel good about themselves while walking away unchanged. He does not care how loud the music is, as long as the Word is absent or watered down.

"For the time will come when they will not endure sound doctrine... they will turn their ears away from the truth and be turned aside to fables." — 2 Timothy 4:3–4

That time is not coming. It is here.

The Rise of Hirelings

Jesus warned of hirelings, leaders who care more about self-preservation than protecting the sheep.

"The hireling sees the wolf coming and leaves the sheep... because he does not care about the sheep." — John 10:12–13

Some pastors today are more concerned with brand than boldness. Their sermons are shaped by algorithms, not the Spirit. They refuse to address controversial topics because controversy might affect attendance, donations, or influence.

But when truth is filtered through fear, the result is compromise.

The deceiver does not tremble at a popular preacher. He trembles at a preacher full of the Holy Spirit, preaching the full counsel of God.

When Churches Redefine Love

The Church is called to love. But love without truth is not love. It is enablement.

Many churches now celebrate what God calls sin. They march with the world while claiming to walk with Christ. They say Jesus affirms rather than transforms.

This is not compassion. It is deception wrapped in Christian language.

Jesus ate with sinners. But He never affirmed their sin. He forgave and said, "Go and sin no more." He loved with truth. He welcomed with conviction. And He called people to holiness.

The deceived church preaches comfort without repentance, grace without surrender, worship without obedience.

And Satan rejoices when churches embrace a love that costs nothing.

The Laodicean Spirit

Jesus warned the Church of Laodicea in the book of Revelation. It was not immoral. It was lukewarm.

"I know your works, that you are neither cold nor hot... So then, because you are lukewarm... I will vomit you out of My mouth." — Revelation 3:15–16

This church was rich in resources, proud of itself, and blind to its spiritual poverty.

Jesus was not inside. He was standing at the door, knocking.

That is where many churches are today. Jesus is not being worshiped. He is being ignored. His Word is not shaping the message. It is being softened to fit modern tastes.

And the enemy is already in the room.

What the Church Must Return To

1. **The Fear of God**
   Reverence must return. God is holy. He is not our mascot. He is not a brand. He is not a product.

2. **The Full Word of God**
   Preach all of it. Not just the comforting parts. Not just the promises. Preach the judgment, the warnings, the cross, and the resurrection.

3. **True Worship**
   Worship that honors God with both the lips and the life. Music with substance. Hearts that tremble at His presence.

4. **Discipleship, Not Just Decisions**
   Churches must stop counting hands raised and start making disciples. We are not called to build crowds. We are called to equip saints.

5. **Boldness in the Spirit**
   Speak truth. Risk offense. Stand firm. If the culture hates it, the Bible probably says it.

The Church Is Still God's Weapon

Not every church is deceived. There is still a remnant. There are still pastors who fear God more than man. There are still churches where truth burns, where repentance is preached, where the power of the Holy Spirit is alive and holy ground is real.

Jesus said the gates of hell would not prevail against His Church.

But that promise was not made to lukewarm religion. It was made to the true, blood-bought, Spirit-filled body of Christ.

The deceiver has infected much. But he cannot stop the Bride of Christ when she is awake, armored, and aligned with heaven.

The Church must rise again—not with new trends, but with ancient truth. Not with marketing, but with message. Not with hype, but with holiness.

Because when the Church preaches the real gospel, the gates of hell shake.

Chapter 11: How to Recognize His Voice

When the Lie Sounds Like Truth

"My sheep hear My voice, and I know them, and they follow Me."
— John 10:27

Satan rarely comes screaming lies. He whispers them.

He does not show up as a monster. He often shows up as a mentor, a friend, a leader, or even a preacher. He wraps his deception in light. He uses familiar phrases, spiritual language, and half-truths that sound right but are deadly.

That is why discernment is no longer optional. It is essential.

You must know how to recognize his voice. Because if you do not, you will be deceived by what feels good, sounds holy, and looks right but leads to ruin.

The Voice of the Deceiver

The devil speaks in patterns. He has a voice. Not a literal one, but a recognizable influence. He has been speaking the same way since Eden.

Here is what his voice often sounds like:

- "Did God really say?"
- "It's not that serious."
- "Everyone does it."
- "God understands your heart."
- "Truth is whatever feels right to you."
- "You're not hurting anyone."
- "You deserve to be happy."

None of these sound evil. That is the point. If Satan showed up with horns and fire, people would run. But when he speaks comfort, self-love, and spiritual-sounding justifications, they follow.

"There is a way that seems right to a man, but its end is the way of death."
— Proverbs 14:12

Deception always has a voice. And you must know how to test it.

When Truth Is Twisted

The devil is a master of misusing Scripture. He quoted the Bible to Jesus in the wilderness. But he left parts out. He took it out of context. He used God's Word for his own agenda.

This still happens today. Verses are isolated. Meanings are changed. Teachers twist grace into permission. Love into lawlessness. Freedom into chaos.

God's Word must be rightly divided. Not everything that uses Scripture honors God. Satan knows the Bible. That is why knowing it for yourself is critical.

"They use the grace of our God as a license for immorality." — Jude 1:4

Discernment is not just knowing the difference between right and wrong. It is knowing the difference between truth and almost truth.

How to Test the Spirit

The Bible tells us clearly what to do.

"Beloved, do not believe every spirit, but test the spirits, whether they are of God." — 1 John 4:1

This means you do not accept every message. You do not follow every voice. You do not trust every dream, every vision, or every teacher.

Here are some biblical tests:

1. Does it agree with the full Word of God?

If it contradicts Scripture, it is not from God. If it requires you to twist, ignore, or downplay any part of the Bible, it is a lie.

2. Does it glorify Jesus or glorify self?

Satan's voice always points to self. God's voice always points to Christ. The Holy Spirit will never lead you away from the Son.

3. Does it convict or merely comfort?

The enemy flatters. The Spirit convicts. God does not speak to affirm your sin. He speaks to transform you.

4. Does it produce holiness?

Truth leads to obedience. The voice of God calls you higher. Satan's voice tells you to relax in disobedience.

5. Does it exalt God's will or your feelings?

God is not guided by emotions. He is unchanging. The deceiver appeals to feelings because feelings change.

The Danger of Familiar Voices

One of Satan's most effective tactics is speaking through voices you trust.

- A friend who says, "Follow your heart."
- A teacher who says, "That part of the Bible no longer applies."
- A preacher who says, "We don't talk about judgment here."

This is why Jesus warned that false prophets would come in sheep's clothing.

You cannot test by appearance. You must test by truth.

"Satan himself transforms himself into an angel of light."
— 2 Corinthians 11:14

He does not just imitate truth. He counterfeits it.

He copies spiritual language. He mimics revelation. He counterfeits anointing. He uses people who appear righteous, but carry a corrupted message.

Know the Shepherd's Voice

Jesus said His sheep know His voice. That means if you are walking with Him, filled with His Spirit, and grounded in His Word, you will recognize what is not from Him.

The more time you spend in truth, the quicker you spot the lie.

You do not need to study every false doctrine. You need to study the real thing until the fake becomes obvious.

Discernment grows in the presence of God. It grows in prayer. It grows through Scripture. It grows when you say no to sin and yes to righteousness.

The voice of the Shepherd is gentle, but clear. He does not flatter. He leads. He does not manipulate. He speaks life. He does not confuse. He brings peace.

"Your Word is a lamp to my feet and a light to my path."
— Psalm 119:105

You Cannot Afford to Be Spiritually Deaf

In an age of constant noise, the greatest danger is that you will become numb to the voice of God. If that happens, the voice of the deceiver will fill the void.

This is not a game. The wrong voice can lead to destruction. The wrong voice can destroy your purpose, your family, your soul.

But the right voice will lead you to life.

You must tune your ears to heaven. You must shut out the noise. You must silence the lies. You must walk so closely with Jesus that when the deceiver speaks, you do not even flinch.

Because you already know it is not the voice of your Shepherd.

Chapter 12: How to Resist the Deceiver

Standing in the Armor of God

"Therefore submit to God. Resist the devil and he will flee from you."
— James 4:7

Satan cannot be reasoned with. He cannot be bargained with. He does not back down because of your intentions. He flees only when he meets resistance from someone fully submitted to God.

You were not meant to be deceived, defeated, or destroyed. You were meant to stand.

But you will not stand in your own strength. You cannot resist the enemy in the flesh. You must be clothed in the full armor of God, armed with truth, and filled with the power of the Holy Spirit.

The deceiver is real. The battle is constant. But you are not powerless.

You have been equipped for victory.

Step One: Submit to God

Before the Bible tells you to resist the devil, it tells you to submit to God.

Submission is the foundation of resistance. You cannot defeat the enemy while still agreeing with him in secret. You cannot walk in authority while living in compromise.

God does not empower rebels. He empowers the surrendered.

Submission means:

- Repenting of hidden sin
- Obeying the Word
- Yielding your will to God's will
- Honoring His Lordship in every area

You cannot wear God's armor if you are still entertaining Satan's lies.

Step Two: Put On the Armor

Paul gives a clear command in Ephesians 6.

"Put on the whole armor of God, that you may be able to stand against the wiles of the devil."

This armor is not optional. It is your survival kit. Each piece is spiritual, but real. It is not symbolic only. It is power.

1. The Belt of Truth

Truth is what holds everything together. Without it, you fall apart. You must know what God has said, or you will believe what Satan says.

Do not build your life on emotion, opinion, or tradition. Build it on Scripture. Wrap yourself in the truth of God's Word every day.

"Sanctify them by Your truth. Your word is truth."
— John 17:17

2. The Breastplate of Righteousness

This is not your righteousness. It is Christ's righteousness given to you by faith.

Righteousness protects your heart. When you walk in obedience, the enemy's accusations lose their power. Holiness is not legalism. It is protection.

"He who practices righteousness is righteous, just as He is righteous."
— 1 John 3:7

3. The Shoes of the Gospel of Peace

You stand firm when you are grounded in the gospel. Peace does not mean comfort. It means confidence. It means you know who you are in Christ and why you are here.

Walk boldly. Speak the gospel. Refuse to be shaken.

"How beautiful are the feet of those who preach the gospel of peace."
— Romans 10:15

4. The Shield of Faith

Faith extinguishes the fiery darts of the wicked one. Doubt is a weapon Satan uses constantly. Faith answers back with trust in God's character and promises.

Do not carry fear. Carry faith. Speak it. Stand in it.

"This is the victory that has overcome the world—our faith."
— 1 John 5:4

5. The Helmet of Salvation

Guard your mind. The battlefield is in your thoughts. Know that you are saved, secured, and sealed by the blood of Jesus.

Do not let the enemy lie to you about your identity or your future.

"Take every thought captive to the obedience of Christ."
— 2 Corinthians 10:5

6. The Sword of the Spirit

This is the only offensive weapon listed. It is the Word of God. You do not just defend with truth. You fight back with it.

Jesus used this sword in the wilderness. So must you. Speak the Word. Declare the Word. Use it as a weapon.

"It is written."
— Matthew 4:4

Step Three: Stay Alert and Pray

Paul follows the armor of God with a powerful instruction.

"Praying always with all prayer and supplication in the Spirit."

You do not just wear the armor. You pray in it. You listen for God's direction. You pray in tongues. You pray with boldness. You pray with persistence.

Prayer is not a ritual. It is warfare.

Satan fears a praying believer more than a preaching one. Because prayer accesses the power of heaven and pushes back the darkness.

Step Four: Stand Your Ground

"Having done all... stand."
— Ephesians 6:13

There will be days when you are not advancing, but you are still standing. And that is victory.

Resisting the devil is not just a moment. It is a posture. It is a lifestyle. Every temptation you overcome is a battle won. Every lie you expose is a chain broken.

Stand in purity. Stand in truth. Stand in identity. Stand in the Spirit.

The enemy wants you to bow, to retreat, to compromise.

But the Word of God says, **stand**.

Step Five: Resist and Watch Him Flee

The Bible is not vague.

"Resist the devil and he will flee from you."

That is a promise.

You do not have to live under attack forever. You do not have to be tormented by lies, bound by fear, or confused by darkness.

When you resist, he flees. When you speak truth, he trembles. When you stand firm in Christ, you are untouchable.

You have authority in Jesus. Not because of who you are, but because of who He is.

"Behold, I give you authority... over all the power of the enemy."
— Luke 10:19

You are not a victim. You are more than a conqueror. But you must fight.

This is not a suggestion. It is survival. This is not metaphor. It is reality.

Put on the armor. Raise your sword. Pray without ceasing.

And let hell know this one is not going down quietly.

Chapter 13: The Final Deception and Ultimate Defeat

The Last War and the End of the Lie

"The devil, who deceived them, was cast into the lake of fire and brimstone... and they will be tormented day and night forever and ever."
— Revelation 20:10

The story of the great deceiver does not end with him victorious. It ends with him judged. From Eden to today, Satan has lied, tempted, corrupted, and destroyed. He has mocked truth, twisted Scripture, and led billions into rebellion against God. But there is coming a day when the deceiver will deceive no more.

His final deception is approaching. His final war is being prepared. But so is his final defeat.

The end is not uncertain. The Bible has spoken.

The Rise of Global Deception

Revelation tells of a time when Satan will empower a man called the beast, or Antichrist. This man will rise to power through deception, flattery, and control. He will be praised by the world. He will be empowered by hell.

"The whole world marveled and followed the beast."
— Revelation 13:3

This final world ruler will not come with horns. He will come with solutions. He will promise peace, unity, and a new era for humanity. He will perform signs. He will speak with power. He will command global worship.

And the world will obey.

But behind the charisma is a lie. Behind the system is a serpent.

This is the devil's final attempt to dethrone God by ruling the hearts of men.

The Mark of the Beast

Scripture describes a time when people will be required to receive a mark on their hand or forehead. Without it, they will not be able to buy or sell.

"He causes all... to receive a mark... that no one may buy or sell except one who has the mark or the name of the beast." — Revelation 13:16–17

This is not just economic control. It is spiritual allegiance. The mark is not about survival. It is about surrender.

Those who take it will align themselves with the beast. Those who refuse will be hunted, hated, and killed.

The deceiver will frame it as unity. As safety. As progress. But it will be the ultimate act of rebellion.

The False Prophet

Alongside the Antichrist, there will be a religious leader empowered by Satan. This man will perform miracles. He will point people to the beast. He will demand worship.

"He performs great signs... he deceives those who dwell on the earth by those signs." — Revelation 13:13–14

This is the final form of false religion. It will blend the languages of all faiths. It will call for tolerance. It will exalt man. But it will deny the one true God.

And many will be led astray.

The War to End All Wars

The Bible describes a final conflict, Armageddon. The armies of the earth will gather to fight against the Lamb. Satan will influence kings. Demons will stir nations. Weapons will be aimed at heaven.

But the outcome will not be a battle. It will be a sentence.

"These will make war with the Lamb, and the Lamb will overcome them." — Revelation 17:14

Jesus will return, not as the suffering Servant, but as the conquering King. With fire in His eyes and a sword from His mouth. Every eye will see Him. Every knee will bow.

And the deceiver will fall.

Satan's Final Judgment

The devil's fate is sealed. He will be bound. He will be silenced. He will be judged. And finally, he will be thrown forever into the lake of fire.

"The devil, who deceived them, was cast into the lake of fire… forever and ever."

This is justice. This is closure. This is the end of the lie.

There will be no more temptation. No more accusation. No more deception. No more war.

The deceiver will not rise again.

The Victory of Christ

Jesus is not losing. He never has. Every move Satan makes is allowed by God for a greater purpose. Every lie will be answered by truth. Every scheme will be crushed by sovereignty. Christ wins. Eternally.

He will wipe every tear. Heal every wound. Restore what was broken. And reign forever.

"The kingdoms of this world have become the kingdoms of our Lord and of His Christ."

— Revelation 11:15

You Must Decide Before the End

The final deception will be powerful. But the Bible says those who love the truth will not be deceived.

God is not hiding. He is calling. He is warning. He is saving.

The door is still open. But it will not stay open forever.

Today is the day to choose.

- Will you follow the truth or the lie?
- Will you stand with Christ or be swept away by the world?
- Will you live for eternity or for the moment?

The great deceiver has written his playbook. But God has already written the final page.

The serpent will not win. The dragon will not rule. The liar will not stand.

Jesus is King.

Forever.

Conclusion: Don't Be Deceived

The Hour Is Late. The War Is Real. The Truth Still Stands.

"Let no one deceive you by any means."
— 2 Thessalonians 2:3

This is not a story. This is not theory. This is not fiction.

The deceiver is real. His work is global. His tactics are ancient. And his grip on the world is growing stronger by the day.

You have just read how Satan fell. How he twisted truth. How he built systems of rebellion. How he infected religion. How he whispers through culture. How he disguises himself as light. How he deceives in 2025. How he invades the Church. How he blinds the lost. How he lies to the saved.

But more importantly, you have also read this:

He does not win.

The Lie That Still Kills

Satan's greatest weapon has never been violence. It has always been the lie. He has convinced millions that sin is freedom, that good is evil, and that God is either too far away to matter or too loving to judge.

He has made deception look like progress. He has rebranded rebellion as enlightenment. He has wrapped destruction in beauty.

And too many have followed him blindly into ruin.

You must not be one of them.

"Be sober, be vigilant, because your adversary the devil walks about like a roaring lion, seeking whom he may devour."
— 1 Peter 5:8

The Truth That Still Saves

There is one weapon Satan cannot overcome. There is one name he cannot stand against. There is one message that breaks chains and shatters lies.

The gospel of Jesus Christ.

Jesus came to destroy the works of the devil. He lived without sin. He died in your place. He rose in power. And He is coming again.

The truth is not an idea. It is a person. His name is Jesus.

"You shall know the truth, and the truth shall make you free." — John 8:32

He does not deceive. He delivers. He does not condemn the sinner who repents. He welcomes them with open arms. He does not offer comfort in darkness. He brings people into the light.

You do not have to be trapped by the deceiver any longer. You can be free.

Final Warnings

- If you are compromising with sin, the deceiver has already spoken to you.
- If you believe all religions lead to God, the deceiver has already clouded your mind.
- If you are numb to spiritual truth, the deceiver has already dulled your ears.
- If you are playing church but not walking with Christ, the deceiver already has your attention.

This is not said to shame you. It is said to awaken you.

Satan does not need to turn you into a Satanist. He only needs to keep you comfortable, distracted, and indifferent.

Final Call

This book was not written to entertain. It was written to sound an alarm.

You are living in the final chapters of history. You are watching prophecy unfold in real time. You are standing at the edge of eternity.

And the deceiver is not done yet.

But neither is God.

"And now, little children, abide in Him, that when He appears, we may have confidence and not be ashamed before Him at His coming." — 1 John 2:28

Abide in Christ. Know the Word. Walk in the Spirit. Resist the lie. Refuse the compromise. Reject the darkness. Renounce every false gospel.

And above all cling to the truth.

The Victory Belongs to Jesus

The devil has had his moment. He has had his schemes. But his time is running out.

Christ is returning. Justice is coming. Truth will reign.

And every knee whether in heaven, on earth, or under the earth will bow.

Not to the deceiver.

But to the Lamb who was slain.

Final Prayer

A Prayer for Truth, Courage, and Deliverance

Heavenly   Father,

In a world full of lies, we come to You for truth. In the face of darkness, we look to Your light. In the presence of deception, we cling to Your Word.

Lord, we confess that we have not always seen clearly. We have listened to voices that did not come from You. We have followed paths that led us away. But today, we return. We submit. We surrender. We stand.

Open our eyes, Lord. Sharpen our discernment. Give us boldness to speak, humility to obey, and strength to resist the enemy.

Clothe us in Your armor. Fill us with Your Spirit. Anchor us in Your truth. And when the deceiver comes with his lies, let our hearts echo Your Word "It is written."

We pray for those still trapped in deception. Break the chains. Expose the lies. Shine Your light into their darkness. Bring revival to Your Church. Purify Your Bride.

Jesus, You are the Way, the Truth, and the Life. Let every heart that reads this book find You. Let no one be lost to the schemes of the enemy.

Let us live for Your glory. Let us endure to the end. Let us never be deceived.

In   the   mighty   name   of   Jesus   Christ, Amen.

Gospel Invitation

Seek the Lord While He May Be Found

Maybe you read this book and realized for the first time that you have been living in deception. Maybe you believed in a version of Christianity that was empty. Maybe you were told lies about who God is. Maybe you were never told anything at all.

Wherever you are right now whether in church or far from it know this:

God sees you. God loves you. And God is calling you.

The Bible says all have sinned. That includes you. That includes me. We have all broken God's law, ignored His truth, and gone our own way.

But God sent His Son, Jesus Christ, to save us. He lived without sin. He died for yours. He rose from the grave. He conquered the deceiver and offers you eternal life not through religion, not through good works, but through faith in Him.

You don't need to clean yourself up before coming to Him. You don't need to have all the answers. What you need is to believe the gospel and call on His name.

"Whoever calls on the name of the Lord shall be saved." — Romans 10:13

Right now, wherever you are, cry out to Him. Confess your sin. Believe He died for you. Surrender your life to Him. Ask Him to fill you with His Holy Spirit, to make you new, and to lead you in truth.

And then **find a Bible-believing, truth-preaching, Christ-exalting church.** Not a place that entertains you. A place that equips you. Not a place that avoids hard truths. A place that lives by them. Ask God to guide you to it. He will.

Open your Bible. Start reading the Gospel of John. Then read Romans. Then read Ephesians. Let God's Word become your foundation. Learn to recognize His voice and walk in His power.

You do not need to stay in darkness. You do not need to remain confused. You do not need to live under lies.

Jesus is truth. He is calling. Say yes.

Made in the USA
Columbia, SC
28 August 2025

61791034R00038